# Understanding and Overcoming LGBT Challenges

## C. P. Kumar
Reiki Healer & Author
Roorkee - 247667, India

# Disclaimer

While every effort has been made to ensure the accuracy and completeness of the content in this book, the author cannot guarantee that the information contained herein is error-free, up-to-date, or suitable for every individual circumstance.

The author shall not be held liable or responsible for any errors or omissions in the content of the book, nor for any damages, or losses that may arise from any actions taken based upon the suggestions or contents presented in the book.

Readers are advised to use their own judgment and discretion in applying the information provided in this book, and to consult with qualified professionals before taking any action based on the contents of this book. The author disclaims any and all liability or responsibility for any actions taken or not taken based on the information contained in this book.

# DEDICATION

To all those who have bravely shared their stories, fought for equality, and paved the way for a more inclusive world,

This book is dedicated to the LGBTQ+ community, whose resilience, strength, and unwavering spirit have sparked movements, challenged norms, and transformed societies.

May the narratives within these pages serve as a testament to the power of authenticity, compassion, and solidarity. In the face of adversity, your voices have echoed with courage, your struggles have illuminated paths toward justice, and your victories have inspired generations to come.

With deepest gratitude and admiration,

C. P. Kumar

# CONTENTS

# PREFACE

In recent decades, the world has witnessed remarkable strides towards recognizing and affirming the rights and dignity of the LGBT community. Yet, despite significant progress, the journey towards full equality and acceptance remains fraught with challenges, hurdles, and deeply ingrained biases. It is within this complex landscape that this book, "Understanding and Overcoming LGBT Challenges", finds its purpose.

Within the pages of this volume, we embark on a multifaceted exploration of the experiences, struggles, and triumphs of LGBT individuals across the globe. From personal narratives of coming out to the intricate intersections of identity, from legal battles for recognition to the fight against discrimination, each chapter delves into a distinct aspect of the LGBT experience.

Our journey begins with an introductory overview of the rich tapestry of the LGBT community, tracing its history, diversity, and evolving terminology. We delve into intimate coming out stories, witnessing the courage and vulnerability of individuals navigating the complexities of self-discovery and societal acceptance.

Throughout this book, we confront the harsh realities of bullying, discrimination, and violence faced by LGBT individuals, both in their daily lives and within legal frameworks. We shine a light on the disparities in healthcare, the prevalence of mental health challenges, and the insidious practice of conversion therapy that seeks to erase identities.

Yet, amidst the adversity, we find resilience, solidarity, and hope. We explore the joys and struggles of building families, the pivotal role of inclusive education and supportive environments, and the intricate dynamics of religious and cultural acceptance.

From media representation to international perspectives, from youth homelessness to the challenges of aging, each chapter illuminates a facet of the LGBT experience, inviting readers to engage critically, empathetically, and compassionately.

As we navigate these narratives, we are reminded not only of the battles fought and the progress achieved but also of the work that lies ahead. In every story of struggle, we find seeds of activism, seeds that have blossomed into movements for change, equality, and justice.

It is our sincere hope that this book serves as a catalyst for understanding, empathy, and dialogue. May it challenge preconceptions, inspire action, and foster a world where every individual, regardless of sexual orientation or gender identity, is embraced for who they are.

In closing, let us remember that the journey towards equality is not a destination but a continuous, collective endeavor - one that requires courage, compassion, and unwavering solidarity.

Together, let us strive towards a future where love, acceptance, and respect transcend boundaries, where the rights and dignity of every human being are cherished and upheld.

C. P. Kumar
Reiki Healer, Blogger & Author

## The Origins of LGBT Identity

The LGBT community, an acronym for Lesbian, Gay, Bisexual, and Transgender, represents a diverse group of individuals who share common experiences related to sexual orientation, gender identity, and expression. The roots of LGBT identity can be traced back throughout history, with evidence of same-sex relationships and gender diversity found across various cultures and civilizations.

In ancient societies such as Greece and Rome, same-sex relationships were not uncommon, and individuals often expressed fluidity in their sexual and gender identities. Similarly, indigenous cultures around the world recognized and honored individuals who identified outside of traditional gender norms.

However, it wasn't until the late 19th and early 20th centuries that the modern LGBT rights movement began to take shape. The Stonewall Riots of 1969 in New York City, sparked by the police raid on the Stonewall Inn, a popular gay bar, marked a pivotal moment in LGBT history. This event galvanized the community to organize and advocate for equal rights, leading to the emergence of numerous LGBT advocacy groups and organizations.

## Understanding Diversity Within the LGBT Community

One of the defining characteristics of the LGBT community is its diversity. While the acronym LGBT encompasses a broad spectrum of identities, it is important to recognize that individuals within the community may identify with additional labels such as queer, intersex, asexual, pansexual, and more.

Moreover, the LGBT community is not homogenous, and individuals within it come from diverse cultural, racial, ethnic, and socioeconomic backgrounds. Understanding and celebrating this diversity is essential in creating an inclusive and supportive environment for all members of the community.

**Terminology and Definitions**

Navigating the terminology and definitions associated with the LGBT community can be complex, especially for those who are not familiar with its nuances. Here are some key terms and definitions to help clarify.

Lesbian: A woman who is emotionally, romantically, or sexually attracted to other women.

Gay: A term often used to describe men who are attracted to other men, though it can also be used more broadly to encompass all individuals attracted to the same gender.

Bisexual: Refers to individuals who are attracted to both men and women.

Transgender: A term used to describe individuals whose gender identity differs from the sex assigned to them at birth.

Queer: An umbrella term used by some individuals to describe sexual orientations and gender identities that do not conform to societal norms.

Intersex: Refers to individuals born with variations in sex characteristics that do not fit typical definitions of male or female.

Asexual: Refers to individuals who do not experience sexual attraction to others.

Pansexual: Refers to individuals who are attracted to people regardless of their gender identity or expression.

It is important to use language that respects and acknowledges individuals' self-identified gender identities and sexual orientations.

**Challenges Faced by the LGBT Community**

Despite significant progress in recent decades, the LGBT community continues to face numerous challenges, including discrimination, prejudice, and violence. Discrimination based on sexual orientation and gender identity remains prevalent in various aspects of life, including employment, housing, healthcare, and education.

LGBT individuals are more likely to experience mental health issues such as depression, anxiety, and substance abuse as a result of societal stigma and rejection. Moreover, transgender individuals, in particular, face disproportionate rates of violence and harassment, with trans women of color being among the most vulnerable.

Legal protections for LGBT individuals vary widely across different jurisdictions, and many continue to advocate for comprehensive nondiscrimination laws at the local, state, and federal levels.

**Overcoming Challenges Through Understanding and Acceptance**

While the challenges facing the LGBT community are significant, progress has been made through increased visibility, advocacy, and allyship. Allies, individuals who support and advocate for LGBT rights, play a crucial role in creating inclusive and affirming spaces for LGBT individuals.

Education and awareness are key components of overcoming discrimination and prejudice. By promoting understanding and acceptance of diverse sexual orientations and gender identities, we can work towards building a more equitable and inclusive society for all.

**Conclusion**

The LGBT community is a vibrant and diverse group of individuals who have historically faced significant challenges in their pursuit of equality and acceptance. By acknowledging the complexities of LGBT identity, promoting inclusivity, and advocating for social and legal change, we can work towards a more just and equitable future for all members of the community.

## Introduction

Coming out, the process by which individuals reveal their sexual orientation or gender identity to others, is a pivotal moment in the lives of many LGBT individuals. It is a deeply personal journey that often involves navigating fear, uncertainty, and vulnerability. Each coming out story is unique, shaped by personal experiences, cultural backgrounds, and societal attitudes towards LGBT identities. In this article, we explore the diverse narratives of individuals as they share their experiences of coming out to their families, friends, and communities.

## The Decision to Come Out

The decision to come out is not one that is made lightly. For many LGBT individuals, it is a complex and emotionally charged process. Some individuals may grapple with their identity for years before finally deciding to come out, while others may feel compelled to do so more spontaneously. The decision to come out is influenced by a variety of factors, including personal readiness, familial and social support networks, and the perceived risks and consequences of disclosure.

## Coming Out to Family

Coming out to family members can be one of the most challenging aspects of the coming out process. Family dynamics, cultural beliefs, and religious affiliations can all impact how families respond to a loved one's disclosure of their LGBT identity. For some individuals, coming out to their families is met with acceptance, love, and support. For others, it can lead to rejection, misunderstanding, and even hostility. The fear of rejection and the desire for acceptance often weigh heavily on individuals as they consider coming out to their families.

## Coming Out Story 1

Sarah, a 23-year-old college student, spent years grappling with her sexuality before deciding to come out to her conservative Christian family. Despite her fears of rejection, Sarah knew she couldn't continue hiding her true self. With trembling hands and a racing heart, she sat her parents down one evening and tearfully revealed that she was gay. Their initial shock turned into silence, and then her father spoke softly, "We love you, Sarah, no matter what". While they struggled to reconcile their beliefs with her identity, Sarah's family eventually came to accept and embrace her, reaffirming their unconditional love.

## Coming Out Story 2

Ryan, a 35-year-old professional, spent years hiding his true identity as a bisexual man due to fear of rejection and judgment from his conservative community. Despite being married to a woman, Ryan struggled with feelings of guilt and shame about his bisexuality. After much soul-searching, he decided to come out to his wife, unsure of how she would react. With trembling hands, he sat her down one evening and tearfully confessed his truth. To his surprise, his wife responded with compassion and understanding, reassuring him that she loved him unconditionally. Together, they embarked on a journey of openness and honesty, navigating the complexities of their relationship with newfound empathy and support.

Thes stories showcase the internal struggle many individuals face in reconciling their sexual orientation or gender identity with societal expectations and personal relationships. It highlights the importance of honesty and communication in fostering understanding and acceptance within intimate partnerships.

**The Role of Friends**

Friends often play a crucial role in the coming out process. They can provide a supportive network of acceptance, understanding, and affirmation for individuals as they navigate their identities. Many LGBT individuals find solace and strength in the friendships they have formed within the LGBT community and among allies. However, coming out to friends is not without its challenges, as individuals may fear losing friendships or facing discrimination and stigma from those they once considered close companions.

Coming Out Story 3

Alex, a transgender man, faced numerous challenges as he prepared to come out to his friends and colleagues at work. Fearful of discrimination and rejection, he carefully planned his disclosure, seeking support from LGBT advocacy groups and allies within the company. When the day finally arrived, Alex gathered his courage and announced his gender transition to his colleagues during a staff meeting. To his relief and surprise, the room erupted in applause and words of encouragement. His coworkers rallied around him, offering unwavering support and respect as he embarked on this deeply personal journey of self-discovery and authenticity.

## Community Support and Acceptance

Community support and acceptance can have a profound impact on an individual's coming out experience. LGBT-friendly spaces, organizations, and events can provide individuals with a sense of belonging and solidarity. Coming out within a supportive community can foster feelings of empowerment, pride, and self-acceptance. However, not all communities are welcoming or inclusive of LGBT individuals. Discrimination, prejudice, and stigma within communities can pose significant barriers to the coming out process and contribute to feelings of isolation and alienation.

Coming Out Story 4

Jasmine, a 28-year-old transgender woman, struggled with her gender identity for years before finding the courage to come out to her friends and seek support from her local LGBT community. Growing up in a small conservative town, Jasmine felt isolated and misunderstood, fearing rejection from her peers and family. However, upon moving to a more diverse city, she discovered a vibrant LGBT community center that provided resources, counseling, and a safe space for individuals like her.

With trepidation, Jasmine attended her first support group meeting, where she was met with warmth and acceptance from fellow transgender individuals and allies. Encouraged by their stories of resilience and empowerment, Jasmine gradually began to embrace her true identity and find the confidence to come out to her friends and family. Despite facing challenges and discrimination along the way, Jasmine found strength and solidarity within her community, knowing that she was not alone in her journey towards self-acceptance and authenticity.

This story underscores the transformative power of community support and acceptance in empowering individuals to embrace their identities and navigate the challenges of coming out. It highlights the importance of inclusive spaces and resources in fostering resilience and belonging within the LGBT community.

**Overcoming Challenges**

Despite the challenges and obstacles they may face, many LGBT individuals find strength and resilience in their coming out journeys. They draw upon their inner courage, determination, and sense of self-worth to navigate difficult conversations, confront prejudice and discrimination, and advocate for their rights and dignity. Coming out is not a one-time event but an ongoing process of self-discovery, self-acceptance, and self-expression.

**Celebrating Identity**

For many individuals, coming out is a transformative experience that allows them to embrace and celebrate their authentic selves. It is a declaration of pride, courage, and defiance in the face of societal norms and expectations. Coming out is not just about disclosing one's sexual orientation or gender identity; it is about reclaiming agency, autonomy, and visibility in a world that often seeks to silence and marginalize LGBT voices.

**Conclusion**

Coming out stories are as diverse and multifaceted as the individuals who share them. They are stories of courage, resilience, and authenticity in the face of adversity. They remind us of the power of love, acceptance, and understanding in creating inclusive and affirming spaces for all individuals, regardless of sexual orientation or gender identity. As we listen to and honor these stories, we reaffirm our commitment to creating a world where everyone can live openly, authentically, and without fear of judgment or discrimination.

## Introduction

Intersectionality is a concept that illuminates the complex interplay of various social identities, such as race, gender, sexual orientation, socioeconomic status, and more. Coined by legal scholar Kimberlé Crenshaw in 1989, intersectionality emphasizes the interconnected nature of oppression and discrimination. In the context of the LGBT community, understanding intersectionality is crucial for grasping the diverse experiences and challenges faced by individuals who belong to multiple marginalized groups. This article delves into the nuances of intersectionality within the LGBT community, exploring how factors like race, gender, and socioeconomic status intersect with LGBT identities.

## Understanding Intersectionality

At its core, intersectionality acknowledges that individuals hold multiple identities simultaneously, and these identities intersect to shape their experiences and social positions. For instance, a black transgender woman experiences discrimination not only based on her gender identity but also due to her race and socioeconomic background. These intersecting axes of identity influence how she navigates the world and interacts with systems of power and privilege.

## Race and LGBT Experiences

The intersection of race and LGBT identities introduces unique challenges and experiences. People of color within the LGBT community often face compounded forms of discrimination and marginalization. Historical and systemic racism exacerbates inequalities faced by LGBTQ+ individuals of color, manifesting in disparities in healthcare access, employment opportunities, housing, and representation in mainstream media and within the LGBT movement itself.

For example, black queer individuals may encounter prejudice and exclusion within predominantly white LGBT spaces, where their experiences and perspectives are often overlooked or marginalized. Additionally, the intersections of racism and homophobia/transphobia can contribute to higher rates of homelessness, unemployment, and violence among LGBTQ+ people of color.

**Gender Identity and Expression**

Gender identity and expression intersect with LGBT experiences in profound ways. Non-binary, transgender, and gender non-conforming individuals navigate a world that often enforces rigid gender norms and binaries. Transgender individuals may face discrimination and violence not only based on their gender identity but also due to societal expectations regarding masculinity and femininity.

Moreover, transgender individuals of color face heightened levels of discrimination and violence, reflecting the intersection of racism, transphobia, and sexism. Access to gender-affirming healthcare, legal recognition of gender identity, and employment protections remain significant challenges for transgender and gender non-conforming individuals, particularly those from marginalized communities.

## Socioeconomic Status and LGBT Identities

The intersection of socioeconomic status with LGBT identities highlights the economic disparities and barriers faced by many within the community. LGBT individuals from low-income backgrounds often encounter limited access to healthcare, housing insecurity, and employment discrimination. Economic marginalization intersects with other forms of oppression, exacerbating vulnerability and limiting opportunities for social mobility.

For instance, LGBT youth experiencing homelessness due to family rejection or discrimination face heightened risks of exploitation, violence, and mental health challenges. Additionally, economic barriers can restrict access to affirming healthcare services, support networks, and legal resources, further perpetuating cycles of poverty and marginalization within the LGBT community.

## Intersectional Advocacy and Solidarity

Addressing the intersecting forms of oppression faced by the LGBT community requires intersectional approaches to advocacy and social change. Recognizing the diverse experiences and needs of individuals within the community is essential for fostering inclusive spaces and amplifying marginalized voices. Intersectional advocacy involves centering the experiences of those most marginalized, challenging systemic inequalities, and building coalitions across diverse communities.

Moreover, solidarity between different social movements, such as racial justice, gender equity, and economic justice, is vital for advancing intersectional perspectives and addressing root causes of oppression. Collaborative efforts aimed at dismantling intersecting systems of power and privilege can create more equitable and inclusive societies for all individuals, regardless of their intersecting identities.

**Conclusion**

Intersectionality serves as a critical framework for understanding the complex intersections of identity and oppression within the LGBT community. By examining how factors like race, gender, and socioeconomic status intersect with LGBT experiences, we gain insight into the diverse challenges faced by individuals who belong to multiple marginalized groups. Moving forward, fostering intersectional advocacy and solidarity is essential for creating inclusive environments and addressing systemic inequalities that impact the lives of LGBT individuals across intersecting identities.

## Introduction

Bullying, discrimination, and hate crimes against LGBT individuals remain prevalent issues in societies worldwide. Despite significant progress in recognizing and affirming the rights of LGBT individuals, they continue to face various forms of harassment and violence solely based on their sexual orientation, gender identity, or expression. Understanding the root causes, dynamics, and impact of bullying and discrimination against LGBT individuals is crucial in fostering inclusive communities and promoting equality for all.

## Understanding Bullying and Discrimination

Bullying and discrimination against LGBT individuals encompass a range of behaviors, from verbal abuse and physical violence to systemic marginalization and exclusion. Bullying can occur in various settings, including schools, workplaces, and public spaces, perpetuating feelings of fear, shame, and isolation among LGBT individuals. Discrimination, on the other hand, involves unequal treatment and opportunities based on one's LGBT status, denying them the right to live authentically and without prejudice.

## Impact on Mental Health and Well-being

The persistent experience of bullying and discrimination takes a significant toll on the mental health and well-being of LGBT individuals. Studies consistently show higher rates of depression, anxiety, substance abuse, and suicidal ideation among LGBT youth and adults who have experienced bullying and discrimination. The internalization of negative societal attitudes and the fear of rejection often lead to profound psychological distress and a diminished sense of self-worth among LGBT individuals.

## Intersectionality and Multiple Forms of Discrimination

It is essential to recognize the intersectionality of identities and the compounded effects of discrimination faced by LGBT individuals who belong to marginalized communities. LGBT people of color, individuals with disabilities, and those from low-income backgrounds often encounter intersecting forms of discrimination based on race, ethnicity, disability, or socioeconomic status, exacerbating their vulnerability to bullying and hate crimes. Intersectional approaches are crucial in addressing the unique challenges faced by diverse LGBT populations and promoting inclusive practices that honor the complexity of human experiences.

## Challenges in Educational Settings

Schools should ideally be safe and nurturing environments for all students, regardless of their sexual orientation or gender identity. However, LGBT youth frequently encounter hostile school climates characterized by harassment, exclusion, and inadequate support from peers and educators. The lack of inclusive curriculum, policies, and resources further marginalizes LGBT students and perpetuates harmful stereotypes and misconceptions. Educators play a pivotal role in creating affirming school environments and implementing policies that promote diversity, equity, and inclusion for all students.

**Workplace Discrimination and Employment Inequality**

Despite advancements in workplace diversity and inclusion initiatives, discrimination against LGBT individuals persists in many professional settings. LGBT employees often face subtle forms of discrimination, such as microaggressions, stereotyping, and unequal treatment in hiring, promotion, and compensation practices.

*Stereotyping* means oversimplified and often unfair assumptions made about individuals or groups based on their perceived characteristics, traits, or attributes. *Microaggressions* refer to subtle, often unintentional, verbal, behavioral, or environmental slights or insults that communicate derogatory or negative messages to individuals or groups based on their race, gender, sexual orientation, ethnicity, or other marginalized identities.

Fear of discrimination and harassment may compel LGBT individuals to conceal their identities at work, compromising their authenticity and sense of belonging in the workplace. Employers must adopt inclusive policies, training programs, and support networks to foster inclusive workplace cultures that celebrate diversity and value LGBT contributions.

**Addressing Hate Crimes and Violence**

Hate crimes targeting LGBT individuals represent the most extreme form of discrimination and intolerance in society. These acts of violence not only inflict physical harm but also instill fear and insecurity within LGBT communities. Transgender individuals, especially transgender women of color, are disproportionately affected by hate-motivated violence and face alarming rates of homicide and assault. Combating hate crimes requires comprehensive legal protections, law enforcement training, and community-led initiatives that prioritize the safety and well-being of LGBT individuals and hold perpetrators accountable for their actions.

## Building Supportive Communities and Allies

Creating inclusive communities that affirm and celebrate LGBT identities is essential in combatting bullying and discrimination. Allies, including family members, friends, colleagues, and community leaders, play a crucial role in advocating for LGBT rights, challenging prejudice, and promoting understanding and acceptance. Supportive networks and resources, such as LGBT-affirming organizations, helplines, and online communities, offer vital support and solidarity to individuals facing discrimination and harassment. By fostering empathy, solidarity, and collective action, communities can create spaces where all individuals feel valued, respected, and empowered to live authentically.

## Conclusion

Bullying, discrimination, and hate crimes against LGBT individuals represent significant challenges that undermine the principles of equality and human dignity. Addressing these issues requires a multifaceted approach that addresses root causes, promotes awareness and understanding, and advocates for legal protections and social change. By fostering inclusive environments, challenging prejudice, and building supportive communities and allies, we can work towards a world where all individuals, regardless of their sexual orientation or gender identity, can live free from fear, discrimination, and violence. It is only through collective action and solidarity that we can overcome the challenges faced by LGBT individuals and create a more just and equitable society for future generations.

## Introduction

The fight for equal rights and recognition has been a cornerstone of the LGBT (Lesbian, Gay, Bisexual, and Transgender) movement for decades. While significant progress has been made in many parts of the world, legal challenges persist, posing hurdles to full equality and acceptance. This article delves into some of the key legal challenges faced by the LGBT community, including marriage equality, adoption rights, and employment discrimination.

## Marriage Equality

One of the most prominent legal battles in recent history has been the fight for marriage equality. Historically, same-sex couples faced discrimination and were denied the right to marry in many countries. However, through advocacy, litigation, and public opinion shifts, significant strides have been made in recognizing the right of same-sex couples to marry.

The landmark case of Obergefell v. Hodges in the United States, decided by the Supreme Court in 2015, legalized same-sex marriage nationwide. This decision was a watershed moment, affirming that the right to marry is a fundamental right guaranteed to all individuals, regardless of sexual orientation.

Despite advancements in many countries, challenges to marriage equality persist in regions where conservative attitudes and legal barriers remain entrenched. In some nations, same-sex marriage is still not recognized, leaving

LGBT couples without the legal protections and benefits afforded to heterosexual couples.

**Adoption Rights**

Another critical legal challenge facing the LGBT community is the right to adopt children. Historically, LGBT individuals and couples have encountered obstacles and discrimination when seeking to adopt or foster children. Legal frameworks governing adoption vary widely across jurisdictions, and in some cases, sexual orientation or gender identity has been used as grounds for denial.

While progress has been made in recognizing the ability of LGBT individuals and couples to provide loving and stable homes for children, discriminatory practices persist in certain regions. Advocates continue to push for reforms to ensure that adoption decisions are based on the best interests of the child rather than outdated biases or prejudices.

**Employment Discrimination**

Employment discrimination based on sexual orientation or gender identity remains a pervasive issue affecting the LGBT community. Despite advances in anti-discrimination laws in many countries, LGBT individuals still face discrimination and harassment in the workplace.

In numerous jurisdictions, there are no explicit protections against discrimination based on sexual orientation or gender identity. This lack of legal safeguards leaves LGBT employees vulnerable to unfair treatment, including being fired, denied promotions, or subjected to hostile work environments simply because of who they are or whom they love.

Efforts to enact comprehensive anti-discrimination legislation have been met with resistance in some regions, highlighting the ongoing struggle for equal rights and workplace protections for LGBT individuals. Advocacy groups and legal experts continue to push for stronger legal safeguards to ensure that all workers are treated fairly and equitably, regardless of sexual orientation or gender identity.

**Transgender Rights**

Transgender individuals face unique legal challenges related to gender identity recognition, access to healthcare, and protection from discrimination. Many legal systems have been slow to adapt to the needs and rights of transgender people, leading to a myriad of legal hurdles and barriers to full inclusion and equality.

Legal recognition of gender identity remains a contentious issue in numerous jurisdictions, with restrictive requirements and bureaucratic hurdles making it difficult for transgender individuals to obtain accurate identity documents that reflect their gender identity. Access to gender-affirming healthcare and appropriate medical treatment is also a significant concern, with many transgender individuals facing discrimination and denial of care.

Moreover, transgender individuals often experience disproportionate levels of violence, harassment, and discrimination in various aspects of life, including employment, education, housing, and healthcare. Efforts to combat these injustices and secure legal protections for transgender people are ongoing, as advocates work to promote equality, dignity, and respect for all gender identities.

**Intersectionality and Legal Advocacy**

It is essential to recognize that the legal challenges faced by the LGBT community intersect with other forms of discrimination and marginalization, including race, ethnicity, socioeconomic status, and disability. Intersectional approaches to legal advocacy seek to address the complex and overlapping forms of oppression experienced by individuals who hold multiple marginalized identities.

For example, LGBT people of color may face compounded discrimination and barriers to accessing legal rights and protections. Similarly, individuals with disabilities within the LGBT community may encounter additional challenges in navigating legal systems and asserting their rights.

Intersectional advocacy efforts aim to address these intersecting forms of discrimination and promote inclusive legal frameworks that recognize the diverse experiences and needs of all members of the LGBT community. By centering the voices and experiences of marginalized individuals, legal advocates can work towards more equitable and inclusive legal systems that uphold the rights and dignity of all people.

**Conclusion**

The legal challenges faced by the LGBT community are multifaceted and complex, requiring ongoing advocacy, education, and legal reform to achieve full equality and inclusion. From marriage equality and adoption rights to employment discrimination and transgender rights, the fight for LGBT rights continues on multiple fronts.

While significant progress has been made in many parts of the world, there is still much work to be done to dismantle systemic barriers and ensure equal treatment under the law for all individuals, regardless of sexual orientation or gender identity. By working together and advocating for change, we can create a more just and inclusive society where all members of the LGBT community can live openly, authentically, and free from discrimination.

## Introduction

Healthcare disparities have long been a critical issue worldwide, affecting various marginalized communities, including the Lesbian, Gay, Bisexual, and Transgender (LGBT) community. Despite advancements in healthcare, members of the LGBT community continue to face unique challenges and disparities in accessing quality healthcare services. This article delves into the disparities faced by the LGBT community in healthcare and underscores the importance of LGBTQ-inclusive care.

## Understanding Healthcare Disparities

Healthcare disparities refer to differences in healthcare access, utilization, quality, and outcomes among various population groups. These disparities are influenced by numerous factors, including socioeconomic status, geographic location, race, ethnicity, gender identity, and sexual orientation.

## Challenges Faced by the LGBT Community

The LGBT community encounters several barriers to accessing adequate healthcare, including discrimination, stigma, lack of cultural competence among healthcare providers, and legal barriers. Discrimination and stigma can lead to fear, reluctance to seek medical care, and avoidance of disclosing sexual orientation or gender identity to healthcare providers.

## Lack of LGBTQ-Inclusive Care

One of the primary challenges faced by the LGBT community is the scarcity of LGBTQ-inclusive healthcare services. Many healthcare providers lack training in addressing the specific healthcare needs of LGBT individuals, leading to inadequate or inappropriate care. This lack of cultural competence can result in misunderstandings, misdiagnoses, and substandard treatment.

## Mental Health Disparities

Members of the LGBT community are at a higher risk of experiencing mental health issues such as depression, anxiety, and suicidality compared to the general population. Minority stress, resulting from societal stigma, discrimination, and lack of acceptance, contributes significantly to mental health disparities among LGBT individuals. However, accessing culturally competent mental healthcare remains a challenge for many in the community.

## Sexual and Reproductive Health

LGBT individuals often encounter barriers to accessing sexual and reproductive healthcare services. Many healthcare providers may not be knowledgeable about the specific sexual health needs of LGBT individuals, including HIV prevention, contraception, and fertility options. Moreover, transgender individuals may face additional challenges in accessing gender-affirming healthcare services, including hormone therapy and gender-affirming surgeries.

**HIV/AIDS and STI Prevention**

The LGBT community, particularly gay and bisexual men, transgender individuals, and men who have sex with men (MSM), are disproportionately affected by HIV/AIDS and other sexually transmitted infections (STIs). Despite advancements in prevention and treatment, stigma and discrimination continue to hinder HIV testing, treatment adherence, and access to preventive measures such as pre-exposure prophylaxis (PrEP) among LGBT individuals.

*Pre-exposure prophylaxis* (PrEP) refers to a preventive treatment regimen where individuals at high risk of contracting a specific infection, notably HIV, take medication regularly to reduce their chances of infection before potential exposure to the virus.

**Barriers to Healthcare Access**

Several systemic barriers contribute to healthcare disparities within the LGBT community, including lack of legal protections, insurance coverage exclusions, and financial constraints. Many LGBT individuals face difficulties accessing healthcare due to discrimination in healthcare settings, denial of services, and lack of culturally competent providers.

**Importance of LGBTQ-Inclusive Care**

Addressing healthcare disparities among the LGBT community requires a multifaceted approach that emphasizes LGBTQ-inclusive care. LGBTQ-inclusive care involves creating safe, welcoming, and affirming healthcare environments where LGBT individuals feel respected, understood, and valued. Healthcare providers must undergo training to enhance their cultural competence and understanding of LGBT-specific health needs.

## Training and Education

Training healthcare providers in LGBTQ cultural competency is essential for improving healthcare outcomes among LGBT individuals. Education should include topics such as sexual orientation and gender identity diversity, LGBT health disparities, effective communication strategies, and best practices for providing inclusive care. By fostering a supportive and inclusive healthcare environment, providers can enhance patient trust, satisfaction, and overall health outcomes.

## Policy and Advocacy

Policy interventions are critical for addressing healthcare disparities and promoting LGBTQ-inclusive care. Advocacy efforts should focus on enacting nondiscrimination laws, expanding insurance coverage for LGBT-specific healthcare services, and integrating LGBTQ health curricula into medical education programs. By advocating for policy changes at the local, state, and national levels, stakeholders can help dismantle systemic barriers to healthcare access for the LGBT community.

## Community Engagement

Engaging with LGBT community organizations and advocacy groups is essential for identifying healthcare needs, raising awareness about available resources, and promoting health equity. Community-based initiatives, support groups, and outreach programs play a vital role in connecting LGBT individuals with culturally competent healthcare providers and supportive services.

## Conclusion

Healthcare disparities remain a significant challenge for the LGBT community, undermining their access to quality healthcare and contributing to adverse health outcomes. Addressing these disparities requires a concerted effort from healthcare providers, policymakers, educators, and community stakeholders. By promoting LGBTQ-inclusive care, advocating for policy changes, and fostering collaboration within the healthcare system, we can work towards achieving health equity for all members of the LGBT community.

## Introduction

The LGBT community has long faced significant challenges, including societal stigma, discrimination, and a lack of acceptance. These factors contribute to higher rates of mental health issues within the community. Understanding the root causes and providing support are crucial steps toward addressing these challenges.

## Understanding Mental Health in the LGBT Community

The LGBT community experiences disproportionately higher rates of mental health issues compared to the general population. Research consistently shows that individuals who identify as lesbian, gay, bisexual, transgender, or queer are more likely to experience depression, anxiety, substance abuse, and suicidal ideation.

## Social Stigma and Discrimination

Social stigma and discrimination play a central role in the mental health disparities faced by the LGBT community. Throughout history, individuals who identify as LGBT have been subjected to prejudice, discrimination, and violence due to their sexual orientation or gender identity. Such experiences can lead to internalized shame, low self-esteem, and psychological distress.

## Family Rejection and Isolation

Family rejection is a significant issue faced by many LGBT individuals. Coming out to family members can result in rejection, alienation, and even homelessness for some individuals. The lack of familial support can exacerbate feelings of loneliness and isolation, contributing to poor mental health outcomes.

## Intersectionality

It's important to recognize the intersectionality of identities within the LGBT community. Factors such as race, ethnicity, socioeconomic status, and disability intersect with sexual orientation and gender identity, shaping individuals' experiences and access to resources. Intersectional approaches are essential in understanding and addressing the unique mental health needs of diverse LGBT populations.

## Transgender and Non-binary Experiences

Transgender and non-binary individuals face distinct challenges related to mental health. Gender dysphoria, discrimination, and barriers to accessing affirming healthcare services are common experiences within this segment of the LGBT community. Supportive environments and access to gender-affirming care are critical for the mental well-being of transgender and non-binary individuals.

## The Importance of Support

Supportive environments and social networks play a vital role in promoting mental health and well-being within the LGBT community. Acceptance, validation, and affirmation of one's identity are fundamental aspects of support that can buffer against the negative impacts of stigma and discrimination.

## Community and Peer Support

Community and peer support networks provide LGBT individuals with a sense of belonging and validation. Through these networks, individuals can connect with others who share similar experiences, fostering solidarity and resilience. Peer support groups, online communities, and LGBT-affirming spaces offer opportunities for individuals to seek guidance, share resources, and access affirming support systems.

## Counseling and Mental Health Services

Access to competent and culturally sensitive mental health services is essential for addressing the mental health needs of the LGBT community. Mental health professionals who are knowledgeable about LGBT issues can provide affirming care that validates individuals' identities and experiences. Counseling services, support groups, and helplines offer avenues for LGBT individuals to seek assistance and professional guidance during times of distress.

## Advocacy and Policy Change

Advocacy efforts aimed at combating discrimination, promoting equal rights, and advocating for LGBT-affirming policies are crucial for improving the mental health outcomes of the LGBT community. Policies that protect against discrimination in employment, healthcare, housing, and education can create safer and more inclusive environments for LGBT individuals to thrive.

**Education and Awareness**

Education and awareness initiatives play a vital role in challenging stereotypes, dispelling myths, and promoting understanding of LGBT issues. By fostering empathy and allyship, education efforts can help reduce stigma and create more supportive communities for LGBT individuals.

**Conclusion**

The higher rates of mental health challenges experienced by the LGBT community are multifaceted and rooted in societal stigma, discrimination, and lack of acceptance. Addressing these challenges requires a comprehensive approach that includes support networks, access to affirming healthcare services, advocacy for policy change, and education to promote understanding and acceptance. By working together to create more inclusive and supportive environments, we can help improve the mental health and well-being of all members of the LGBT community.

## Introduction

Conversion therapy, also known as reparative therapy or sexual orientation change efforts (SOCE), refers to practices aimed at changing an individual's sexual orientation or gender identity. Despite numerous condemnations from medical and psychological associations worldwide, conversion therapy persists in various forms across different cultures and societies. This article delves into the harmful effects of conversion therapy on LGBT individuals, highlighting its origins, methods, and the psychological toll it exacts.

## Understanding Conversion Therapy

Conversion therapy traces its roots back to early psychoanalytic theories that pathologized homosexuality as a mental disorder. Sigmund Freud, often regarded as the father of psychoanalysis, viewed homosexuality as a deviation from normal development, contributing to the stigmatization of non-heteronormative identities. These beliefs laid the foundation for therapeutic interventions aimed at altering sexual orientation and gender identity.

*Non-heteronormative identities* encompass sexual orientations, gender identities, and relationship structures that do not conform to the traditional societal expectations and assumptions of heterosexuality as the norm. This includes identities such as homosexuality, bisexuality, pansexuality, asexuality, transgender identities, and various forms of non-binary and genderqueer identities, as well as alternative relationship models like polyamory and open relationships.

## Methods and Techniques

Conversion therapy employs a range of methods and techniques, including talk therapy, aversion therapy, and religious interventions. Talk therapy sessions often involve attempts to uncover underlying trauma or family dynamics presumed to have caused the individual's non-heterosexual orientation. Aversion therapy utilizes negative stimuli, such as electric shocks or nausea-inducing drugs, to associate same-sex attractions with discomfort or pain. Religious interventions rely on prayer, scripture readings, and religious counseling to 'pray the gay away' or suppress transgender identities under the guise of spiritual healing.

## The Harmful Impact on LGBT Individuals

Conversion therapy inflicts profound psychological harm on LGBT individuals, exacerbating feelings of shame, guilt, and self-loathing. By pathologizing their innate identities, conversion therapy perpetuates internalized homophobia and transphobia, leading to heightened anxiety, depression, and suicidal ideation. The relentless pressure to conform to heteronormative standards erodes self-esteem and undermines the individual's sense of authenticity and self-worth.

*Homophobia and transphobia* are forms of discrimination, prejudice, and hostility directed towards individuals or groups based on their sexual orientation or gender identity, respectively. Homophobia specifically targets individuals who are homosexual or perceived to be homosexual, while transphobia targets individuals who are transgender or perceived to be transgender. These attitudes can manifest in various forms, including verbal abuse, harassment, physical violence, and societal marginalization, and they contribute to systemic inequalities and violations of human rights for LGBTQ+ individuals.

*Heteronormative standards* are societal norms, expectations, and assumptions that prioritize and reinforce heterosexuality as the normative or preferred sexual orientation. These standards often dictate and influence various aspects of life, including relationships, family structures, social interactions, cultural representations, and institutional policies. Heteronormativity can marginalize or invalidate non-heterosexual identities and relationships, perpetuating discrimination and inequality based on sexual orientation.

Moreover, the coercive nature of conversion therapy violates fundamental principles of autonomy and consent. Many individuals subjected to conversion therapy are minors coerced into treatment by their parents or guardians, who may be influenced by societal prejudices or religious beliefs. This lack of agency and control over one's own identity compounds the trauma experienced during conversion therapy sessions, fostering feelings of helplessness and alienation from one's true self.

## Legal and Ethical Considerations

In recent years, there has been a growing recognition of the ethical and human rights implications of conversion therapy. Numerous professional associations, including the American Psychological Association and the World Psychiatric Association, have issued statements condemning the practice as ineffective, harmful, and unethical. Several countries and jurisdictions have enacted legislative measures to ban or restrict conversion therapy, recognizing it as a form of psychological abuse and a violation of human rights.

Despite these advancements, conversion therapy remains prevalent in many parts of the world, fueled by deeply entrenched social prejudices and religious dogma. Advocates of conversion therapy often cite religious freedom and parental rights as justification for their practices, disregarding the irreparable harm inflicted on LGBT individuals in the process. Efforts to combat conversion therapy require a multifaceted approach that encompasses legislative reform, public education, and advocacy for LGBT-inclusive healthcare policies.

**Moving Towards Affirmative Therapy**

In contrast to conversion therapy, affirmative therapy embraces principles of acceptance, support, and empowerment for LGBT individuals. Affirmative therapy seeks to create a safe and affirming environment where clients can explore and embrace their authentic identities free from judgment or shame. Therapists trained in affirmative approaches utilize affirmative language, validate the client's experiences, and address the unique challenges faced by LGBT individuals in a heteronormative society.

Central to affirmative therapy is the recognition of sexual orientation and gender identity as natural and diverse aspects of human experience. Rather than pathologizing non-heteronormative identities, affirmative therapy celebrates the richness and complexity of human sexuality and gender expression. By fostering self-acceptance and resilience, affirmative therapy equips LGBT individuals with the tools to navigate societal stigma and discrimination while cultivating meaningful connections within their communities.

## Conclusion

Conversion therapy represents a grave violation of human dignity and a stark reminder of the enduring struggles faced by LGBT individuals in their quest for acceptance and equality. As we strive to create a more inclusive and affirming society, it is imperative that we confront the harmful legacy of conversion therapy and advocate for policies and practices that uphold the rights and dignity of all individuals, regardless of sexual orientation or gender identity. Through education, activism, and solidarity, we can work towards a future where every individual is celebrated for who they are, free from the shackles of prejudice and discrimination.

## Introduction

Transgender rights have been a focal point in discussions surrounding equality and human rights. Transgender individuals face unique challenges that stem from societal norms, discrimination, and systemic barriers. In this article, we delve into the specific hurdles transgender individuals encounter, focusing on access to healthcare, legal recognition, and social acceptance.

## Understanding Transgender Healthcare

Access to adequate healthcare is a fundamental right, yet transgender individuals often face barriers when seeking medical assistance. The healthcare system frequently lacks sensitivity and knowledge regarding transgender-specific needs. From routine check-ups to transition-related care, transgender individuals encounter discrimination, ignorance, and sometimes outright denial of services.

*Transition-related care* refers to medical, psychological, and social interventions provided to individuals undergoing gender transition. These interventions aim to help transgender and gender non-conforming individuals align their gender identity with their physical appearance and/or social roles. Transition-related care may include hormone therapy, gender-affirming surgeries, mental health support, voice therapy, legal assistance with name and gender marker changes, and other forms of support to help individuals achieve their desired gender expression and improve their overall well-being.

One significant challenge is the lack of transgender-affirming healthcare professionals. Many medical practitioners lack training in transgender healthcare, leading to misgendering, inappropriate treatment, and even refusal to provide necessary care. This deficiency in understanding exacerbates the already prevalent mistrust within the transgender community towards healthcare systems.

Moreover, insurance coverage for transgender-related healthcare remains inadequate or non-existent in many regions. Transition-related treatments such as hormone therapy and gender-affirming surgeries are often deemed cosmetic or elective, leaving transgender individuals to bear the financial burden themselves.

*Hormone therapy* and *gender-affirming surgeries* are two primary components of medical transition care for transgender and gender non-conforming individuals.

Hormone therapy: Hormone therapy involves the administration of hormones, such as testosterone or estrogen, to align an individual's physical characteristics with their gender identity. For transgender men (assigned female at birth), testosterone therapy can induce masculinizing effects like voice deepening, facial hair growth, and body hair growth. For transgender women (assigned male at birth), estrogen therapy can induce feminizing effects such as breast development, fat redistribution, and softer skin.

Gender-affirming surgeries: Gender-affirming surgeries, also known as sex reassignment surgeries or gender-confirming surgeries, are surgical procedures that alter a person's physical characteristics to align them with their gender identity. These surgeries can include procedures such as chest reconstruction (mastectomy or breast augmentation), genital reconstruction (vaginoplasty, phalloplasty, metoidioplasty), facial feminization surgery, and other procedures tailored to individual needs and goals.

Both hormone therapy and gender-affirming surgeries are crucial components of gender transition for many transgender individuals, helping to alleviate gender dysphoria and improve overall well-being and quality of life. However, not all transgender individuals pursue or require these medical interventions as part of their transition journey, and the decision to undergo such treatments is highly individualized and based on personal needs and preferences.

**Legal Recognition and Documentation**

Legal recognition is essential for affirming transgender individuals' identities and ensuring their rights are upheld in society. However, obtaining accurate identification documents that reflect one's gender identity can be a daunting task. Many jurisdictions require extensive, invasive, and costly processes for gender marker changes on official documents.

The lack of standardized procedures across regions adds to the complexity. Some areas demand proof of medical transition, while others mandate surgical interventions that not all transgender individuals desire or can afford. This creates significant barriers for those who cannot conform to such requirements due to personal, medical, or financial reasons.

Furthermore, the absence of legal recognition exposes transgender individuals to discrimination and harassment in various settings, including employment, education, and travel. Misgendering and outing can occur when identification documents do not align with one's gender presentation, leading to distress and potential safety concerns.

*Misgendering* refers to the act of using language or pronouns that do not accurately reflect a person's gender identity. It often involves referring to someone using pronouns, titles, or terms that do not align with their gender identity, which can be hurtful, disrespectful, and invalidating to the individual's identity.

*Outing* refers to revealing someone's sexual orientation or gender identity without their consent, often exposing them to potential harm, discrimination, or social consequences. Outing can occur intentionally or unintentionally and can have serious repercussions for the individual's safety, relationships, and well-being.

Both misgendering and outing are harmful practices that undermine the dignity and autonomy of LGBTQ+ individuals. It is important to respect and affirm people's gender identities and sexual orientations and to refrain from disclosing personal information about others without their explicit consent.

**Social Acceptance and Inclusion**

Despite growing awareness and advocacy efforts, transgender individuals continue to face stigma and marginalization in society. Discrimination manifests in various forms, including verbal abuse, physical violence, and institutionalized prejudice. Transphobia (irrational fear, prejudice, or discrimination against transgender and gender non-conforming individuals), rooted in ignorance and fear, perpetuates harmful stereotypes and perpetuates a hostile environment for transgender people.

One of the primary challenges is the lack of acceptance within families and communities. Many transgender individuals experience rejection, estrangement, and abandonment from loved ones when they come out or express their gender identity. This lack of familial support can have severe consequences on one's mental health, leading to depression, anxiety, and suicidal ideation.

Educational institutions, workplaces, and public spaces also struggle to provide inclusive environments for transgender individuals. Bullying, harassment, and exclusionary policies create barriers to education, employment, and participation in social activities. The absence of transgender-inclusive policies and support networks further isolates transgender individuals and denies them equal opportunities for growth and fulfillment.

**Overcoming Challenges and Promoting Transgender Rights**

Addressing the specific challenges faced by transgender individuals requires concerted efforts from various stakeholders, including policymakers, healthcare providers, educators, employers, and community leaders. Advocacy for transgender rights should be intersectional, recognizing the overlapping oppressions faced by transgender individuals who also belong to marginalized communities based on race, ethnicity, class, disability, and immigration status.

In healthcare, comprehensive training programs for medical professionals on transgender healthcare needs are imperative. This includes education on respectful language, cultural competency, and best practices for providing transgender-affirming care. Healthcare policies must be revised to ensure equitable access to transition-related treatments and insurance coverage for transgender-specific healthcare needs.

Legal reforms are necessary to streamline the process of gender marker changes and ensure that transgender individuals can obtain accurate identification documents without undue hardship. Gender-neutral identification options should be made available to accommodate non-binary and gender non-conforming individuals. Anti-discrimination laws must be strengthened and enforced to protect transgender people from discrimination in all aspects of life.

Promoting social acceptance requires multifaceted approaches that foster understanding, empathy, and allyship within communities. Education campaigns, diversity training, and cultural competency workshops can challenge misconceptions and prejudices surrounding transgender identities. Creating safe spaces and support networks for transgender individuals can mitigate feelings of isolation and provide essential resources for empowerment and resilience.

**Conclusion**

Transgender rights are human rights, and ensuring equality and dignity for transgender individuals is a moral imperative. By addressing the specific challenges faced by transgender individuals in healthcare, legal recognition, and social acceptance, we can move towards a more inclusive and equitable society. It is incumbent upon all of us to advocate for transgender rights, challenge discrimination and prejudice, and create a world where every individual can live authentically and free from fear.

## Introduction

In the realm of family and parenting, the experiences of LGBT individuals reflect a journey of resilience, love, and overcoming unique challenges. In the pursuit of parenthood, whether through adoption, surrogacy, or other means, LGBT individuals navigate societal norms, legal frameworks, and personal aspirations to create loving families. This article delves into the diverse paths taken by LGBT individuals in building families, shedding light on the triumphs and tribulations they encounter along the way.

## The Evolution of LGBT Parenting Rights

The landscape of LGBT parenting has evolved significantly in recent decades, marked by legal advancements and changing societal attitudes. Historically, LGBT individuals faced systemic barriers to parenthood, including discriminatory adoption policies and limited legal recognition of same-sex relationships. However, landmark legal cases and advocacy efforts have led to significant progress, granting LGBT individuals the right to adopt and foster children in many jurisdictions.

## Adoption

Adoption stands as a poignant testament to the resilience of LGBT individuals in their quest for parenthood. Despite strides in legal recognition, same-sex couples and LGBT individuals still encounter obstacles in the adoption process. Discriminatory practices, ingrained biases, and legal ambiguities persist in some regions, impeding the adoption journey for many LGBT hopefuls. Moreover, the process of adoption itself can be emotionally taxing, requiring patience, perseverance, and unwavering commitment.

**Surrogacy**

For LGBT individuals seeking biological parenthood, surrogacy offers a pathway fraught with both promise and complexity. Surrogacy arrangements involve intricate legal agreements, medical procedures, and emotional negotiations, all of which underscore the profound desire for parenthood among LGBT individuals. Despite the logistical challenges, surrogacy empowers LGBT individuals to realize their dreams of biological kinship, forging deep emotional bonds with their children and surrogate partners along the way.

**The Dynamics of Same-Sex Parenting**

The experiences of same-sex parents illuminate the transformative power of love and resilience in the face of societal scrutiny. Same-sex couples navigate a myriad of challenges unique to their family dynamic, from confronting heteronormative expectations to advocating for their children's rights in educational and social settings. Moreover, same-sex parents often grapple with legal ambiguities surrounding parental rights and recognition, underscoring the ongoing struggle for full equality and inclusion in family law.

**Fostering Inclusive Family Environments**

In the journey toward inclusive family environments, education and advocacy play pivotal roles in fostering acceptance and understanding. LGBT parents and their children thrive in communities that celebrate diversity, embrace difference, and challenge traditional notions of family structure. By promoting dialogue, empathy, and cultural competency, society can create nurturing spaces where all families - regardless of sexual orientation or gender identity - can flourish and thrive.

**Overcoming Stigma and Building Resilience**

Despite significant progress, stigma and discrimination continue to cast shadows over the experiences of LGBT families. From microaggressions to systemic barriers, LGBT individuals confront a myriad of challenges in their pursuit of parenthood and familial fulfillment. Yet, in the face of adversity, LGBT parents exemplify unwavering resilience, drawing strength from their love for their children and unwavering commitment to creating inclusive, affirming spaces for future generations.

**The Imperative of Legal Protections and Social Support**

As we look toward the future, the imperative of legal protections and social support for LGBT families looms large on the horizon. Comprehensive legal frameworks, nondiscrimination policies, and culturally competent support services are essential in safeguarding the rights and well-being of LGBT parents and their children. Moreover, ongoing efforts to challenge societal norms, promote visibility, and amplify LGBT voices are crucial in cultivating environments of acceptance and belonging for all families.

**Conclusion**

The experiences of LGBT individuals in building families epitomize the transformative power of love, resilience, and collective action. From adoption to surrogacy, LGBT parents traverse diverse paths in their pursuit of parenthood, confronting challenges and forging new frontiers along the way. As we strive toward a more inclusive society, let us celebrate the rich tapestry of LGBT families, embracing diversity as a cornerstone of familial love and belonging.

## Introduction

In recent years, there has been a growing recognition of the challenges faced by LGBT (Lesbian, Gay, Bisexual, and Transgender) youth in educational settings. Schools, which should ideally be safe and inclusive environments for all students, often fall short in providing adequate support for LGBT youth. This article explores the various obstacles encountered by LGBT students in schools, including bullying, lack of inclusive curriculum, and the critical role of supportive educators in fostering a positive learning environment.

## Understanding Bullying and Harassment

One of the most prevalent challenges faced by LGBT youth in schools is bullying and harassment. Research consistently shows that LGBT students are disproportionately targeted for bullying compared to their heterosexual and cisgender peers. *Cisgender* refers to individuals whose gender identity aligns with the sex they were assigned at birth. Verbal taunts, physical violence, and exclusion from peer groups are all too common experiences for many LGBT students. The consequences of bullying can be severe, leading to decreased academic performance, mental health issues, and even higher rates of dropout among LGBT youth.

Bullying often stems from prejudice, ignorance, and a lack of acceptance of diverse sexual orientations and gender identities. LGBT students may face hostility not only from their peers but also from teachers and other school staff. Hostile school climates contribute to feelings of isolation and alienation among LGBT youth, making it difficult for them to fully engage in their education and thrive academically.

**The Need for Inclusive Curriculum**

Another significant challenge for LGBT youth in educational settings is the lack of inclusive curriculum. Many school curricula fail to adequately address issues related to sexual orientation and gender identity, perpetuating a heteronormative and cisnormative worldview which refer to perspectives that uphold heterosexuality as the norm for sexual orientation and cisgender identities as the standard for gender identity, respectively, often marginalizing or excluding LGBTQ+ individuals and experiences. LGBT students rarely see themselves reflected in the materials they study, which can lead to feelings of invisibility and marginalization.

Inclusive curriculum goes beyond simply acknowledging the existence of LGBT individuals; it incorporates their contributions to history, literature, science, and other academic disciplines. By including diverse perspectives in the curriculum, schools can create a more inclusive learning environment where all students feel valued and respected. Inclusive education not only benefits LGBT students but also promotes understanding and acceptance among their peers.

**The Role of Supportive Educators**

Supportive educators play a crucial role in creating safe and affirming school environments for LGBT youth. Teachers and school staff who are knowledgeable about issues related to sexual orientation and gender identity can serve as allies and advocates for LGBT students. By actively challenging stereotypes, confronting discrimination, and promoting acceptance, educators can help create a culture of inclusivity within their schools.

Supportive educators also provide vital support and resources for LGBT students who may be struggling with their identity or facing harassment from their peers. Establishing Gay-Straight Alliances (GSAs) or similar support groups can provide a sense of community and belonging for LGBT youth. These spaces offer opportunities for students to connect with peers who share similar experiences and to access information and support from trusted adults.

Training and professional development for educators are essential components of creating LGBT-inclusive schools. Educators need the knowledge and skills to address issues related to sexual orientation and gender identity sensitively and effectively. Providing training on topics such as LGBT history, terminology, and support strategies can help educators better understand the needs of their LGBT students and create more supportive learning environments.

**Conclusion**

Creating inclusive and affirming school environments for LGBT youth requires a multifaceted approach that addresses the various challenges they face. From combating bullying and harassment to implementing inclusive curriculum and supporting educators, schools play a pivotal role in promoting the well-being and academic success of LGBT students.

By acknowledging and addressing the unique needs of LGBT youth, schools can foster a culture of acceptance, respect, and diversity. Through advocacy, education, and collaboration, we can work towards a future where all students, regardless of sexual orientation or gender identity, feel safe, supported, and valued in their educational journey. It is only through collective effort and commitment that we can truly overcome the challenges faced by LGBT youth in educational settings and create a more equitable and inclusive society.

## Introduction

In contemporary society, the acceptance and inclusion of LGBT individuals have become defining issues in the realm of human rights and social justice. However, the journey towards acceptance is fraught with numerous challenges, particularly when it comes to the clash between religious beliefs, cultural norms, and the recognition of LGBT rights. This article delves into the intricate dynamics of these conflicts, exploring how religious and cultural perspectives intersect with the acceptance of LGBT individuals.

## Understanding Religious Perspectives

Religious beliefs often play a significant role in shaping attitudes towards LGBT individuals. Many major world religions have doctrines and scriptures that explicitly address homosexuality and gender identity, often framing them within the context of moral codes and divine laws. For instance, in Christianity, interpretations of biblical texts have varied widely, with some denominations embracing LGBT inclusion while others adhere to more traditional interpretations that condemn homosexuality.

Similarly, in Islam, interpretations of the Quran and Hadiths have led to diverse viewpoints on LGBT issues, ranging from outright condemnation to more nuanced approaches that emphasize compassion and understanding. Other religious traditions, such as Judaism, Hinduism, and Buddhism, also grapple with reconciling ancient teachings with contemporary understandings of human sexuality and gender diversity.

## Cultural Norms and Traditions

Cultural norms and traditions exert a profound influence on societal attitudes towards LGBT individuals. In many cultures, notions of gender roles, family structures, and social expectations are deeply ingrained, often intersecting with religious teachings to form a complex tapestry of beliefs and values. In some cultures, the mere discussion of LGBT identities remains taboo, with individuals facing ostracism, discrimination, and even violence for openly expressing their sexual orientation or gender identity.

Moreover, cultural attitudes towards LGBT individuals can vary widely across different regions and communities, reflecting the diversity of human experiences and historical contexts. While some cultures have a long history of recognizing and accepting non-binary gender identities, others adhere rigidly to binary conceptions of gender and sexuality, leaving little room for deviation or exploration.

## Conflicts and Challenges

The intersection of religious beliefs, cultural norms, and LGBT acceptance often gives rise to conflicts and challenges that impact individuals, families, and communities. One of the primary sources of conflict stems from the perceived clash between religious teachings and LGBT rights, with some religious leaders and institutions actively opposing efforts to promote equality and non-discrimination.

For LGBT individuals who come from devoutly religious backgrounds, the process of coming out and asserting their identities can be fraught with emotional turmoil and rejection. Many face pressure to conform to traditional gender roles and heterosexual norms, leading to feelings of alienation and self-doubt. In some cases, individuals may be subjected to conversion therapies or other forms of religiously motivated interventions aimed at changing their sexual orientation or gender identity.

Moreover, families and communities often grapple with the challenge of reconciling their religious and cultural values with the lived experiences of LGBT loved ones. Interpersonal relationships may be strained, as parents, siblings, and extended family members struggle to accept and affirm the identities of their LGBT relatives. In conservative societies, the fear of social stigma and reputational damage may compel families to prioritize conformity over authenticity, further perpetuating cycles of silence and denial.

**Building Bridges and Fostering Understanding**

Despite the complexities and tensions inherent in the intersection of religious beliefs, cultural norms, and LGBT acceptance, there are also opportunities for dialogue, reconciliation, and mutual respect. Building bridges between religious communities and LGBT advocates is essential for fostering understanding and promoting social change.

Interfaith dialogue initiatives bring together representatives from diverse religious traditions to engage in respectful and constructive conversations about LGBT issues. By highlighting shared values of compassion, justice, and human dignity, these dialogues create space for exploring common ground and challenging prejudice and discrimination.

Similarly, grassroots movements within religious communities are working to promote greater acceptance and inclusion of LGBT individuals. Progressive religious leaders and organizations advocate for interpretations of scripture that affirm the inherent worth and dignity of all people, regardless of sexual orientation or gender identity. Through education, advocacy, and community outreach, these efforts help to challenge stereotypes and promote a more inclusive understanding of faith and spirituality.

Cultural shifts are also underway in many parts of the world, as attitudes towards LGBT individuals evolve and societies become more open to diversity and difference. Through art, literature, media, and popular culture, voices from the LGBT community are gaining greater visibility and representation, challenging stereotypes and promoting empathy and understanding.

**Legal and Policy Considerations**

Legal and policy frameworks play a crucial role in shaping the rights and protections afforded to LGBT individuals in different contexts. In many countries, laws governing marriage, adoption, employment, and healthcare have historically discriminated against LGBT people, denying them equal access to opportunities and services.

However, significant progress has been made in recent years towards advancing LGBT rights through legislative and judicial reforms. The decriminalization of homosexuality, the recognition of same-sex marriage, and the implementation of anti-discrimination laws are important milestones in the struggle for equality and justice.

Nevertheless, challenges persist, particularly in regions where religious conservatism and cultural resistance to LGBT rights remain entrenched. Legal battles over issues such as bathroom access, religious exemptions, and hate crime legislation underscore the ongoing struggle to secure full recognition and protection of LGBT rights under the law.

*Bathroom access* refers to the ability of individuals to use public restrooms and facilities that align with their gender identity, ensuring their right to privacy, dignity, and safety while accessing essential amenities.

**Conclusion**

The conflicts between religious beliefs, cultural norms, and the acceptance of LGBT individuals are complex and multifaceted, reflecting deep-seated attitudes and historical legacies. While progress has been made in advancing LGBT rights globally, significant challenges remain in reconciling diverse perspectives and fostering greater understanding and acceptance.

By promoting dialogue, fostering empathy, and advocating for legal and policy reforms, individuals and communities can work towards building a more inclusive and equitable society where all people, regardless of sexual orientation or gender identity, are valued and respected. It is through collective action and solidarity that we can overcome the barriers to LGBT acceptance and create a world where diversity is celebrated and embraced.

## Introduction

In contemporary society, the media plays a significant role in shaping perceptions, attitudes, and understanding of various social groups, including the LGBT (Lesbian, Gay, Bisexual, Transgender) community. Media representations of LGBT individuals have evolved over time, reflecting changing societal norms, legal advancements, and cultural shifts. However, despite progress, mainstream media often perpetuates stereotypes and lacks diverse and authentic portrayals of LGBT individuals. This article delves into the complexities of media representation, analyzes prevailing stereotypes, and underscores the urgent need for more inclusive narratives.

## The Evolution of LGBT Representation

The portrayal of LGBT individuals in mainstream media has undergone a transformative journey. Historically, LGBT characters were either invisible or depicted through negative stereotypes, relegated to peripheral roles, or portrayed as villains or objects of ridicule. Early representations often reinforced societal prejudices and stigmatized LGBT identities. However, with the rise of LGBTQ+ activism and advocacy, media depictions gradually began to evolve, albeit slowly.

In the late 20th and early 21st centuries, groundbreaking films, television shows, and literature emerged, challenging conventional norms and humanizing LGBT experiences. Works such as "Brokeback Mountain", "Philadelphia", and "Angels in America" offered nuanced portrayals of LGBT characters, highlighting their struggles, triumphs, and humanity. These milestones paved the way for increased visibility and acceptance, contributing to greater social awareness and empathy.

**Stereotypes in Mainstream Media**

Despite progress, mainstream media continues to perpetuate harmful stereotypes and misconceptions about LGBT individuals. One prevalent stereotype is the portrayal of gay men as effeminate, flamboyant, and promiscuous, while lesbians are often depicted as masculine or predatory.

Effeminate: Describes behaviors, mannerisms, or traits that are perceived as traditionally feminine or characteristic of women. In the context of gay men, it often refers to the expression of qualities or interests that deviate from stereotypical masculinity.

Flamboyant: Refers to a person who is ostentatious, colorful, and exuberant in their behavior, appearance, or mannerisms. It is often associated with theatricality and extravagance and can be used to describe individuals, including gay men, who exhibit vibrant or attention-grabbing characteristics.

Promiscuous: Describes engaging in sexual activity with multiple partners or having a casual attitude towards sexual relationships. Historically, gay men have been stereotyped as promiscuous, which has contributed to negative perceptions and stigmatization within society.

Predatory: This term is sometimes misapplied to stereotype or stigmatize individuals based on their sexual orientation or gender identity, which can be harmful and contribute to discrimination.

These caricatures not only oversimplify diverse experiences within the LGBT community but also reinforce harmful gender norms and expectations.

Transgender individuals, in particular, face egregious misrepresentation and erasure in mainstream media. Trans characters are frequently sensationalized, reduced to punchlines, or portrayed as tragic figures grappling with identity crises. Such portrayals fail to capture the complexities of gender identity and perpetuate discrimination and violence against trans people.

Moreover, bisexuality is often rendered invisible or dismissed as a phase, reinforcing the binary understanding of sexual orientation. Bisexual individuals are frequently depicted as indecisive, untrustworthy, or hypersexualized, further marginalizing their experiences within the LGBT spectrum.

**The Impact of Media Representation**

Media representations play a pivotal role in shaping societal attitudes and perceptions towards marginalized communities. For many individuals, media serves as their primary source of information and exposure to diverse identities and experiences. Consequently, inaccurate or stereotypical portrayals can perpetuate prejudice, discrimination, and internalized shame among LGBT individuals.

Negative representations not only harm the self-esteem and mental well-being of LGBT individuals but also contribute to social exclusion and violence. Studies have consistently shown that exposure to negative media depictions correlates with increased levels of prejudice and hostility towards LGBT individuals. Moreover, the lack of authentic representation deprives audiences of the opportunity to empathize with diverse lived experiences and fosters ignorance and indifference.

## The Need for Diverse and Authentic Portrayals

Amidst ongoing strides towards equality and inclusion, the media must prioritize diverse and authentic representations of LGBT individuals. Authenticity entails depicting LGBT characters as multidimensional individuals with agency, aspirations, and flaws, beyond their sexual orientation or gender identity. It necessitates centering diverse voices and narratives that reflect the rich tapestry of LGBT experiences across intersecting identities such as race, class, and disability.

Moreover, media creators and producers must actively engage with LGBT communities, consulting with individuals and organizations to ensure accurate and respectful portrayals. Authentic representation requires sensitivity, empathy, and a commitment to challenging prevailing stereotypes and biases. By amplifying diverse voices and experiences, media can foster empathy, understanding, and solidarity across communities.

## Promising Initiatives and Challenges Ahead

While progress has been made, challenges persist in achieving equitable representation in mainstream media. Limited opportunities, institutionalized homophobia, and censorship pose significant barriers to LGBT inclusion and visibility. Moreover, the commercial imperatives of media industries often prioritize profit over authenticity, perpetuating tokenism and exploitation of LGBT identities for sensationalism.

However, promising initiatives and grassroots movements are reshaping the media landscape, advocating for greater diversity and accountability. The proliferation of digital platforms and independent media has democratized storytelling, providing opportunities for marginalized voices to be heard and amplified. From web series to podcasts, emerging creators are challenging traditional norms and amplifying authentic narratives that defy stereotypes and expand representation.

**Conclusion**

Media representation plays a pivotal role in shaping societal attitudes, perceptions, and understanding of diverse communities, including the LGBT population. While progress has been made in challenging prevailing stereotypes and amplifying diverse voices, mainstream media continues to perpetuate harmful misconceptions and erasure. Authentic representation requires a concerted effort to center diverse narratives, challenge stereotypes, and amplify marginalized voices.

As we navigate towards a more inclusive media landscape, it is imperative for media creators, producers, and consumers to critically examine prevailing narratives and advocate for greater diversity and authenticity. By centering diverse experiences and perspectives, media can serve as a catalyst for empathy, understanding, and social change, fostering a more equitable and inclusive society for all.

## Introduction

Homelessness is a pervasive issue that affects communities worldwide, but among the most vulnerable demographics are LGBT youth. Despite progress in recognizing and protecting the rights of the LGBT community, disparities persist, particularly concerning access to safe housing. In this article, we delve into the complex factors contributing to the disproportionately high rates of homelessness among LGBT youth and advocate for the urgent need for safe housing options.

## Understanding the Disparities

### 1. Socioeconomic Factors

LGBT youth often face rejection from their families and communities, leading to strained relationships and, in many cases, outright expulsion from their homes. This rejection can leave them without financial support or a stable living environment, exacerbating their vulnerability to homelessness.

### 2. Discrimination and Stigma

Discrimination based on sexual orientation or gender identity remains a significant barrier to accessing housing and employment opportunities for LGBT individuals. Prejudice and stigma can lead to systemic marginalization, making it difficult for LGBT youth to secure safe and stable living arrangements.

### 3. Mental Health Challenges

The experience of homelessness can take a severe toll on mental health, exacerbating existing issues or triggering new ones. LGBT youth who are homeless often grapple with feelings of isolation, depression, and anxiety, further complicating their ability to navigate their circumstances and seek help.

### 4. Lack of Support Networks

For many LGBT youth, the absence of supportive networks compounds the challenges they face. Without access to affirming spaces or resources tailored to their unique needs, they may struggle to find assistance and guidance in securing housing and other essential services.

## The Need for Safe Housing Options

### 1. Cultivating Accepting Environments

Creating safe housing options for LGBT youth requires cultivating environments that are affirming, inclusive, and free from discrimination. Housing providers and policymakers must prioritize creating spaces where LGBT individuals feel welcomed, respected, and supported.

### 2. Access to Culturally Competent Services

Service providers must undergo training to ensure they possess the cultural competency needed to address the specific needs and challenges faced by LGBT youth. This includes understanding the nuances of gender identity and sexual orientation and providing appropriate support and resources.

## 3. Collaboration and Partnerships

Addressing homelessness among LGBT youth necessitates collaboration among government agencies, non-profit organizations, advocacy groups, and community stakeholders. By pooling resources and expertise, stakeholders can develop comprehensive strategies and initiatives to combat homelessness and provide safe housing options.

## 4. Empowering LGBT Youth

Empowering LGBT youth involves equipping them with the tools, resources, and support needed to navigate their circumstances and advocate for themselves. This includes providing access to education, employment opportunities, healthcare services, and mentorship programs that foster resilience and self-sufficiency.

## 5. Legal Protections and Advocacy

Advocacy efforts must focus on enacting and enforcing legal protections that safeguard the rights and well-being of LGBT individuals, including protections against housing discrimination based on sexual orientation or gender identity. Additionally, advocacy initiatives can raise awareness of the systemic barriers faced by LGBT youth and mobilize support for policy reforms and social change.

**Conclusion**

The disproportionately high rates of homelessness among LGBT youth underscore the urgent need for action to ensure access to safe and affirming housing options. By addressing the underlying socioeconomic disparities, discrimination, and lack of support networks, we can create environments where LGBT youth feel valued, respected, and supported. Through collaborative efforts, advocacy, and a commitment to justice and equality, we can work towards a future where homelessness among LGBT youth is eradicated, and all individuals have the opportunity to thrive and live authentically.

## Introduction

Aging is a universal process that presents challenges to individuals across various spectrums of society. However, for lesbian, gay, bisexual, and transgender (LGBT) individuals, the aging process can often be compounded by unique challenges. In this article, we delve into the distinctive obstacles faced by older LGBT individuals, focusing particularly on social isolation and inadequate healthcare.

## Understanding the Context

Before delving into the challenges faced by aging and elderly LGBT individuals, it's crucial to understand the historical context that has shaped their experiences. For much of modern history, LGBT individuals have faced systemic discrimination, social stigma, and marginalization. Laws criminalizing same-sex relationships, social ostracism, and medical pathologization of gender identity have been significant factors contributing to the challenges faced by this community.

*Medical pathologization* of gender identity refers to the historical practice of classifying gender diversity, such as transgender identities, as mental disorders within medical and psychiatric frameworks, leading to stigma, discrimination, and harmful treatments.

# 1. Social Isolation

One of the most pervasive issues confronting aging and elderly LGBT individuals is social isolation. This isolation can stem from a variety of factors, including estrangement from family members, loss of social networks due to discrimination, and the invisibility of LGBT elders within mainstream aging services.

## Estrangement from Family

Many LGBT individuals have experienced rejection from their families of origin due to their sexual orientation or gender identity. As they age, this estrangement can become particularly acute, leaving them without the familial support networks that many non-LGBT individuals rely on in their later years.

## Loss of Social Networks

Throughout their lives, LGBT individuals may create social networks within the LGBT community as a means of finding support and understanding. However, as they age, they may experience the loss of these networks due to relocation, illness, or death, leaving them isolated and disconnected from sources of social support.

## Invisibility within Aging Services

Mainstream aging services often lack cultural competency when it comes to serving LGBT individuals. As a result, LGBT elders may feel unwelcome or unseen within these spaces, further exacerbating feelings of isolation and alienation.

## 2. Inadequate Healthcare

Access to adequate healthcare is another significant challenge faced by aging and elderly LGBT individuals. From discriminatory treatment by healthcare providers to a lack of understanding of LGBT-specific health needs, the healthcare system frequently fails to meet the needs of this population.

### Discriminatory Treatment

Studies have shown that LGBT individuals often experience discrimination within healthcare settings, ranging from derogatory language to outright denial of care. For aging and elderly LGBT individuals, this discrimination can be particularly harmful, leading to avoidance of necessary medical treatment and exacerbation of health issues.

### Lack of LGBT-specific Health Services

Many healthcare providers lack training in LGBT cultural competency and may be unaware of the unique health needs of LGBT individuals. As a result, aging and elderly LGBT individuals may struggle to find healthcare providers who are knowledgeable about their specific health concerns, such as hormone replacement therapy for transgender individuals or screening for LGBT-specific cancers.

### Financial Barriers

Financial barriers can also impede access to healthcare for aging and elderly LGBT individuals. Higher rates of poverty among LGBT elders, coupled with limited access to employment and retirement benefits due to systemic discrimination, can make it difficult for this population to afford necessary medical care.

**Addressing the Challenges**

While the challenges faced by aging and elderly LGBT individuals are significant, there are steps that can be taken to address these issues and improve the lives of this population.

## 1. Promoting LGBT-inclusive Aging Services

A key step in addressing social isolation among aging and elderly LGBT individuals is the promotion of LGBT-inclusive aging services. This includes training aging service providers in LGBT cultural competency, creating LGBT-affirming spaces within existing aging services, and actively reaching out to LGBT elders to ensure they feel welcome and supported.

## 2. Increasing LGBT Health Awareness

Healthcare providers must receive training in LGBT cultural competency and awareness of LGBT-specific health issues. This includes understanding the unique health needs of transgender individuals, addressing disparities in access to care among LGBT populations, and creating healthcare environments that are welcoming and affirming for all patients.

## 3. Advocating for Policy Changes

Advocacy at the local, state, and national levels is essential for enacting policy changes that address the needs of aging and elderly LGBT individuals. This includes advocating for nondiscrimination protections in healthcare settings, increasing funding for LGBT-specific aging services, and promoting policies that address the economic disparities faced by LGBT elders.

**Conclusion**

Aging and elderly LGBT individuals face unique challenges, including social isolation and inadequate healthcare. These challenges are rooted in a history of discrimination and marginalization, but by promoting LGBT-inclusive aging services, increasing awareness of LGBT health issues, and advocating for policy changes, we can work towards creating a more equitable and supportive environment for aging and elderly LGBT individuals. As we strive to build a society that values and respects individuals of all sexual orientations and gender identities, it is imperative that we address the needs of this often-overlooked population.

## Introduction

Activism and advocacy have been central to the progress of the LGBT (Lesbian, Gay, Bisexual, and Transgender) community worldwide. Over the decades, the LGBT movement has evolved, facing both triumphs and setbacks in its pursuit of equal rights and societal acceptance. Understanding the history of LGBT activism provides insights into the challenges faced and the remarkable strides made towards equality. This article explores the rich history of LGBT activism, the pivotal moments that have shaped the movement, and the ongoing efforts to overcome challenges and achieve full inclusion and acceptance.

## The Stonewall Riots

The modern LGBT rights movement traces its roots back to the Stonewall Riots of 1969, a watershed moment in LGBT history. Located in New York City's Greenwich Village, the Stonewall Inn was a popular gathering place for the LGBT community. In the early hours of June 28, 1969, a police raid on the Stonewall Inn sparked a series of spontaneous protests and demonstrations by patrons and supporters, lasting several days.

The Stonewall Riots marked a turning point, galvanizing the LGBT community to resist police harassment and societal discrimination. Marsha P. Johnson, Sylvia Rivera, and other transgender activists played significant roles in the uprising, demanding dignity, respect, and equal rights. The legacy of Stonewall continues to inspire activism and solidarity in the fight against oppression and injustice.

**Early Advocacy Efforts and Legal Battles**

Following Stonewall, the LGBT rights movement gained momentum, with activists organizing protests, marches, and advocacy campaigns across the United States and around the world. The 1970s saw the emergence of LGBT organizations such as the Gay Liberation Front and the Gay Activists Alliance, advocating for civil rights, anti-discrimination laws, and societal acceptance.

Legal battles became a crucial battleground for LGBT rights, with landmark cases challenging discriminatory laws and policies. In 1973, the American Psychiatric Association removed homosexuality from its list of mental disorders, a significant victory for LGBT advocates challenging the medicalization of sexual orientation.

**The AIDS Crisis**

The emergence of the AIDS epidemic in the 1980s brought unprecedented challenges to the LGBT community, disproportionately affecting gay and bisexual men, as well as transgender individuals. The lack of government response and societal stigma surrounding HIV/AIDS fueled activism and grassroots organizing within the LGBT community.

Groups like ACT UP (AIDS Coalition to Unleash Power) and Queer Nation emerged as powerful forces, demanding access to healthcare, research funding, and an end to discrimination against people living with HIV/AIDS. The AIDS crisis mobilized diverse communities, fostering alliances and solidarity across racial, gender, and socioeconomic lines.

## Legal Progress and Setbacks

Despite significant progress in the fight for LGBT rights, challenges persisted on both legal and societal fronts. The Defense of Marriage Act (DOMA), enacted in 1996, denied federal recognition of same-sex marriages and relegated LGBT couples to second-class citizenship. However, grassroots organizing and strategic litigation efforts led to incremental victories, paving the way for marriage equality.

In 2003, the landmark Supreme Court case Lawrence v. Texas struck down sodomy laws, decriminalizing consensual same-sex relationships nationwide. The repeal of DOMA in 2013 and the Supreme Court's historic ruling in Obergefell v. Hodges in 2015 legalized same-sex marriage across all fifty states, marking a historic triumph for the LGBT rights movement.

## Transgender Rights and Visibility

While progress has been made in advancing LGBT rights, transgender individuals continue to face systemic discrimination, violence, and marginalization. Transgender rights have emerged as a critical frontier in the fight for equality, with activists advocating for legal protections, healthcare access, and gender-affirming policies.

The visibility of transgender individuals in media, politics, and popular culture has raised awareness of trans issues and challenged harmful stereotypes and misconceptions. Transgender activists and allies are leading efforts to amplify transgender voices, promote inclusive policies, and combat transphobia in all its forms.

**Intersectionality and Inclusive Advocacy**

Intersectionality, a framework that acknowledges the interconnected nature of social identities and systems of oppression, has become increasingly central to LGBT advocacy and activism. Recognizing the diverse experiences and struggles within the LGBT community, intersectional approaches prioritize solidarity, inclusion, and equity for all marginalized groups.

Advocates are working to address the intersecting forms of discrimination faced by LGBT people of color, immigrants, people with disabilities, and other marginalized communities. By centering the voices and experiences of those most affected by systemic injustice, intersectional activism seeks to build coalitions and create lasting social change.

**The Ongoing Struggle for Equality and Acceptance**

Despite significant gains in LGBT rights and visibility, the fight for equality is far from over. Transgender and non-binary individuals continue to face heightened levels of violence, discrimination, and legal barriers to healthcare and employment. LGBT youth are disproportionately at risk of homelessness, bullying, and suicide, highlighting the urgent need for comprehensive support and resources.

In the face of ongoing challenges, grassroots activism, community organizing, and allyship remain essential tools in the pursuit of justice and equality for all. By amplifying diverse voices, challenging systemic injustices, and building inclusive communities, we can continue the legacy of LGBT activism and create a more just and equitable world for future generations.

## Conclusion

Activism and advocacy have been instrumental in advancing the rights and visibility of the LGBT community throughout history. From the Stonewall Riots to the fight for marriage equality and beyond, courageous individuals and grassroots movements have challenged oppression, transformed hearts and minds, and paved the way for progress.

As we reflect on the legacy of LGBT activism, we must remain committed to the ongoing struggle for equality and acceptance. By centering intersectional perspectives, fostering solidarity, and amplifying marginalized voices, we can create a more inclusive society where all individuals are free to live authentically, with dignity, and without fear of discrimination or violence. Together, we can build a future where love, justice, and equality prevail.

## Introduction

In recent years, there has been significant progress in the recognition and acceptance of LGBT (lesbian, gay, bisexual, and transgender) rights in many parts of the world. However, despite this progress, LGBT individuals still face a myriad of challenges, often varying widely depending on the country and culture they live in. Understanding these challenges from an international perspective is crucial for fostering greater awareness and promoting meaningful change.

## Legal and Policy Frameworks

One of the most fundamental challenges faced by LGBT individuals across the globe relates to legal and policy frameworks. In many countries, discriminatory laws and policies persist, ranging from outright criminalization of homosexuality to the absence of legal protections against discrimination based on sexual orientation and gender identity. In some regions, same-sex relationships are still punishable by imprisonment or even death, leading to widespread fear and persecution among LGBT communities.

## Social Stigma and Discrimination

Social stigma and discrimination represent pervasive challenges for LGBT individuals in virtually every corner of the world. Despite growing acceptance in some societies, many LGBT individuals still face prejudice, rejection, and violence from their families, communities, and institutions. This stigma can have profound effects on mental health and well-being, leading to higher rates of depression, anxiety, and suicide among LGBT populations.

## Cultural and Religious Beliefs

Cultural and religious beliefs often play a significant role in shaping attitudes toward LGBT individuals. In some cultures, traditional norms and values perpetuate the marginalization and exclusion of LGBT people, viewing homosexuality and gender diversity as incompatible with cultural or religious teachings. These deeply ingrained beliefs can create formidable barriers to acceptance and equality, posing unique challenges for LGBT individuals seeking recognition and respect within their communities.

## Access to Healthcare

Access to healthcare is another critical issue facing LGBT individuals worldwide. Many LGBT people encounter barriers to accessing quality healthcare services, including discrimination from healthcare providers, lack of culturally competent care, and inadequate support for transgender-specific healthcare needs.

*Culturally competent care* refers to healthcare services that are respectful, responsive, and inclusive of the cultural beliefs, values, practices, and needs of diverse patient populations, aiming to improve health outcomes and reduce disparities.

These disparities contribute to higher rates of certain health conditions among LGBT populations and hinder efforts to address their unique healthcare needs effectively.

**Legal Recognition of Relationships and Families**

The legal recognition of relationships and families is a key challenge for LGBT individuals seeking equality under the law. While some countries have made significant strides in legalizing same-sex marriage and extending adoption rights to LGBT couples, many others still deny recognition to same-sex relationships and families. This lack of legal protection can have far-reaching consequences, affecting inheritance rights, access to healthcare benefits, and parental rights for LGBT individuals and their families.

**Transgender Rights and Gender Identity**

Transgender rights and gender identity represent a distinct set of challenges within the broader LGBT community. Transgender individuals face unique barriers to acceptance and inclusion, including discrimination in employment, housing, and healthcare, as well as challenges related to legal recognition of gender identity and access to gender-affirming care. The intersectionality of gender identity and expression further complicates efforts to address the diverse needs of transgender people worldwide.

**Intersectionality and Multiple Forms of Discrimination**

Intersectionality - the interconnected nature of social categorizations such as race, class, gender, and sexual orientation - underscores the complexity of LGBT challenges worldwide. Many LGBT individuals face intersecting forms of discrimination based on multiple aspects of their identity, exacerbating their vulnerability to marginalization and exclusion. Addressing these intersecting forms of discrimination requires a holistic approach that recognizes the unique experiences and needs of diverse LGBT communities.

## Advocacy and Resistance

Despite the challenges they face, LGBT individuals and their allies around the world continue to advocate for equality, dignity, and human rights. From grassroots activism to international advocacy efforts, the global LGBT rights movement has made significant strides in raising awareness, challenging discriminatory laws and policies, and promoting greater acceptance and inclusion for LGBT individuals. Through collective action and solidarity, advocates strive to create a more just and equitable world for all people, regardless of sexual orientation or gender identity.

## Conclusion

The challenges faced by LGBT individuals in different countries and cultures worldwide are complex and multifaceted, rooted in a combination of legal, social, cultural, and structural factors. While progress has been made in advancing LGBT rights in many parts of the world, significant disparities and injustices persist, requiring sustained efforts to address systemic discrimination and promote greater acceptance and inclusion for LGBT individuals everywhere. By understanding and confronting these challenges from an international perspective, we can work towards a more just and equitable world where all people are free to live authentically and with dignity, regardless of their sexual orientation or gender identity.

## Introduction

As we reach the final chapter of this comprehensive exploration of LGBT challenges, it's essential to conclude on a note of optimism and resilience. Despite the numerous hurdles and adversities faced by the LGBT community, there have been remarkable strides forward, marked by stories of courage, progress, and hope. In this chapter, we delve into the remarkable progress made by the LGBT community and highlight inspiring narratives that embody resilience and hope for a brighter future.

## Celebrating Legal Victories

One of the most significant milestones in the journey towards equality and acceptance has been the legalization of same-sex marriage in many parts of the world. From the groundbreaking Supreme Court decision in the United States to the legalization of same-sex marriage in various countries across Europe and beyond, the recognition of marriage equality has been a watershed moment for the LGBT community. These legal victories not only affirm the rights of LGBT individuals to love and marry whom they choose but also represent a broader societal shift towards inclusivity and acceptance.

## Visibility and Representation in Media

The representation of LGBT individuals in mainstream media has also undergone a transformation in recent years. From critically acclaimed films and television shows featuring diverse LGBT characters to mainstream advertising campaigns that celebrate love in all its forms, there has been a significant increase in visibility and representation. These representations not only challenge stereotypes and promote understanding but also provide role models and affirmation for LGBT individuals around the world.

## Advancements in Healthcare and Mental Health Support

There has been a growing recognition of the unique healthcare needs of the LGBT community, leading to advancements in LGBTQ-inclusive care and support services. From specialized clinics and healthcare providers to mental health resources tailored to the needs of LGBT individuals, there has been a concerted effort to address healthcare disparities and ensure access to quality care for all. Additionally, greater awareness and destigmatization of mental health issues within the LGBT community have led to increased support networks and resources for those in need.

## Empowerment Through Education and Advocacy

Education and advocacy have played a pivotal role in empowering the LGBT community and fostering greater understanding and acceptance. From inclusive curriculum initiatives in schools to grassroots activism and advocacy campaigns, there has been a concerted effort to challenge discrimination and promote equality. Organizations and individuals dedicated to LGBT rights have worked tirelessly to raise awareness, change hearts and minds, and advocate for policies that protect the rights and dignity of LGBT individuals everywhere.

**Stories of Resilience and Hope**

At the heart of the LGBT movement are countless stories of resilience, courage, and hope. From the brave individuals who have come out in the face of adversity to the trailblazers who have fought tirelessly for equality and justice, these stories inspire us and remind us of the strength of the human spirit. Whether it's the transgender youth who finds acceptance and support from their chosen family, the same-sex couple who celebrates their love and commitment surrounded by friends and loved ones, or the activists who march and organize for change, these stories remind us that progress is possible and that hope prevails even in the darkest of times.

**Looking Towards the Future**

As we reflect on the progress made by the LGBT community and the challenges that lie ahead, it is clear that there is much work still to be done. Discrimination, violence, and inequality continue to impact the lives of LGBT individuals around the world, reminding us of the importance of continued advocacy and activism. However, as we look towards the future, we do so with optimism and determination, knowing that the journey towards equality and acceptance is one worth fighting for. Together, we can build a world where every individual, regardless of their sexual orientation or gender identity, can live authentically, free from fear and discrimination.

In closing, let us celebrate the progress made by the LGBT community and draw inspiration from the stories of resilience and hope that have brought us to this moment. As we continue on our journey towards a more inclusive and just society, may we carry forward the lessons learned and the values upheld by the LGBT community, striving always towards a future where love, acceptance, and equality prevail for all.

92

"Understanding and Overcoming LGBT Challenges" delves into the multifaceted landscape of the LGBT community, offering insight and guidance across diverse dimensions. From tracing the historical trajectory to dissecting contemporary issues, this book navigates through critical topics with sensitivity and depth. It begins with an exploration of the community's rich tapestry and terminology before delving into intimate accounts of coming out experiences. Intersectionality is scrutinized, unveiling the layered complexities of identity.

Bullying, discrimination, and legal hurdles are confronted head-on, while healthcare and mental health disparities are underscored. Through poignant narratives, the harmful impacts of conversion therapy are laid bare, while transgender rights and family dynamics are illuminated. Education, religion, media, and homelessness each find their place in this comprehensive discourse, culminating in a global exploration of progress and hope. With a blend of scholarship and empathy, this book amplifies the voices of resilience, fostering understanding and advocacy in pursuit of equality and acceptance.

# ABOUT THE AUTHOR

**Mr. C. P. Kumar** is a retired Scientist 'G' from National Institute of Hydrology, Roorkee, Uttarakhand, India. He is also a Reiki Healer and Chakra Balancing practitioner (with pendulum dowsing) and offers Emotional Freedom Technique (EFT) to help individuals with emotional issues. Mr. Kumar has authored many books on technical, spiritual, and social topics.

For further details, you may visit his webpage
https://www.angelfire.com/nh/cpkumar/virgo.html